Group Counseling

The subtleties of counseling are very difficult to accurately express in written form alone. This is particularly true in the case of group work, where the interpersonal dynamics expand geometrically. A good group counseling textbook, such as the fifth edition of *Group Counseling: Concepts and Procedures* (2013), can provide a solid foundation, but video demonstrations can illustrate the nuances of the group experience in ways that words alone cannot. To provide just such a video, Kevin A. Fall has filmed a series of segments of a group in which he acts as leader with six participants, over the course of which he demonstrates the stages of a group moving from the first session through to termination. Fall offers regular sections of audio commentary, analysis, and processing on each segment, totaling a 120 minute program. The companion workbook provides additional information to fill in what is not shown on the film and includes exercises, activities, and discussion questions related to each video segment. The video and workbook are designed to work seamlessly with the Berg, Landreth, and Fall text, but they can also be used alongside any other group counseling textbook.

Kevin A. Fall, PhD, is Associate Professor of Counseling and Program Coordinator in the Department of Counseling, Leadership, Adult Education, and School Psychology at Texas State University—San Marcos.

Group Counseling

Process and Technique

Kevin A. Fall

Routledge
Taylor & Francis Group

NEW YORK AND LONDON

First published 2013
by Routledge
711 Third Avenue, New York, NY 10017

Simultaneously published in the UK
by Routledge
27 Church Road, Hove, East Sussex BN3 2FA

Routledge is an imprint of the Taylor & Francis Group, an informa business

© 2013 Taylor & Francis

The right of Kevin A. Fall to be identified as author of this work has been
asserted by him in accordance with sections 77 and 78 of the Copyright,
Designs and Patents Act 1988.

ISBN: 978-0-415-64480-8 (pbk)
ISBN: 978-0-203-07908-9 (ebk)
ISBN: 978-0-415-64482-2 (pack)

Typeset in Adobe Caslon and Frutiger
by Florence Production Ltd, Stoodleigh, Devon

SFI Certified Sourcing
www.sfiprogram.org
SFI-00453

Printed and bound in the United States of America
by Edwards Brothers, Inc.

Contents

Preface

"What does a 'good' group look like?" This was a question that I asked as a doctoral student, specializing in group. In my training, I co-facilitated many groups and led group on my own, but the technology did not exist to actually watch people do groups and the only recordings available were not that good, in my opinion. Over the past fifteen years, I have taught graduate group classes and have led or co-led more groups than I can count, and I still hear that question, but this time from my students. In an attempt to answer this undying question, I decided to include this DVD as a supplemental resource for the newest revision of our text, *Group Counseling: Concepts and Procedures*. The new question for me is, "How do I capture group on a DVD?" The process is more challenging than you may believe. Times have changed since my doctoral training and we now possess the technology to film groups in a wide range of ways. There are a few examples on the market, each with their respective pros and cons. To film my group, here are some of the things I considered.

First, to get a sense of real group process, I wanted to film an entire, eight-week group and then make that available, with commentary to the public. By capturing the whole life of a group, everyone could see what a group *really* looks like. The problem? Group professors would groan at having to find sixteen hours of class time to show the group. Either that or I would be asking the professors to watch and edit the group for class purposes. But if you are going to edit it, what is the purpose of filming the entire group? That format is just not workable for teaching. Besides, it would be too expensive to film and package. Thus, the dream of filming an entire group died on the vine.

I thought if I couldn't film an entire group, then maybe a "critical incident" approach would be good. As I consulted colleagues and the literature, what you see here is what I developed. The segments I chose are based on either aspects of group that appear in every group experience (i.e. "First Session," "Preparing for Termination," and "Termination") or elements of group that group leaders should strive to facilitate, but also might struggle with at times (Moving to the Here and Now, Conflict, and greater group member responsibility). Each segment's duration is less than twenty minutes, which allows the viewer to get a good look at the relevant dynamics, but also allows for whatever you need to do in class. I hope you will find it useful.

In doing a project like this, obviously I needed quite a bit of help. First, I would like to thank Bob Berg and Garry Landreth for giving a young doctoral student a shot to work on the third edition of the textbook way back in 1996. That opportunity has opened so many opportunities for me and helped me develop a lifelong passion for group. I can never thank you enough for that and for trusting me to develop this DVD supplement to our text. Thanks also to the students that helped with this project: Mallory Stover, Greg Hinton, Caroline Sweatt, Kurt Pohl, Ritz Valle, and Chali Henderson. I couldn't have done it without you. Lastly, thanks to Dana Bliss, Christopher Tominich, and Fred Coppersmith at Routledge, Elizabeth Robey at Alexander Street Press, and Bob Currie and Salwa Khan at vcYES Productions for their expertise and vision to see this project to completion.

Kevin A. Fall, Ph.D.

How to Use this Workbook

Hello and welcome to *Group Counseling: Process and Technique*, the workbook companion to the DVD. This workbook and DVD are designed to complement the material presented in the textbook, *Group Counseling: Concepts and Procedures* (5th edn) by Berg, Landreth, and Fall. The DVD and the workbook are new to the latest edition and represent an attempt to provide students with a visual example of important incidents in the developmental life of a typical group. By way of introduction, here are the people in the group:

- Dr. Kevin A. Fall, Group Facilitator
- Amanda
- Greg
- Kurt
- Chali
- Caroline
- Mallory.

You will get to know each of them as you watch the segments. It is important to note what this group is and how it formed. The group members are students in a graduate counseling program at Texas State University—San Marcos. They were recruited by Dr. Fall. Each member was given the segment title, developed their own group member style, and met once as a group to discuss the project. The group then met on film day and filmed each segment in order. Although not a "real" group in the traditional sense, the remarkable thing about group is that you cannot fake group dynamics. The interactions are not scripted and what you are viewing represent real examples of people interacting as a group at different stages of the group process.

Before you watch any segment, read the overview to learn about the general dynamics of what you will be seeing and why the segment was selected. Each part was included because it represents a crucial developmental stage of the group process and might include moments in group that cause leaders some difficulty. Answer the "Preview Reflection Questions" as a way to get you thinking about the group processes that will occur in the segment.

As you prepare to watch the DVD, realize that there are several different perspectives from which you can watch the segments. First, you can watch from the leader perspective. If you are like I was during my graduate training, you probably have not had the opportunity to see many actual groups so your models for leadership are limited. When watching from the leader perspective, think about what the leader is doing. How is he interacting with the group? Why does he choose the interventions he selects? What would you do differently? Next, watch from the member perspective. In this view, you are watching the segment as if you were a member in the group. How would you fit into the group? How would you respond to what the leader is doing? How would you respond to each of the other members in the group? Last, you can watch each session as a process observer. In this role, you are trying to see the big picture of the group. Try to identify group dynamics and concepts. Try to delineate between content and process. The three different levels will encourage you to watch the segments at least three different times.

As you watch each segment, it might be a good idea to first watch it without looking at the verbatim. Just view the interactions and get a sense of what is going on in the group. For your second viewing, read along with the verbatim in the workbook. I have included commentary and additional questions for you as you work through the segment. The commentary provides useful process observations of what was going on in group or what the leader was trying to do at crucial moments in the group. Once you have viewed the segment from the various vantage points, you should have a good grasp on the dynamics and have many ideas on how you would have interacted differently with the group. Proceed to the "Reflection Questions" as a way to process and integrate your thoughts and ideas before you begin the next segment.

I am very happy with how this came out. I think all of the segments will provide viewers with many different levels of learning. What I like best about it is that it is not perfect. In reviewing the DVD for this workbook, there are many things I could do differently, but the imperfections mirror what happens in every group. I hope you enjoy watching it.

Overview of the Developmental Stages of Group

A complete discussion of the stages can be found in Chapter 8 of the *Group Counseling: Concepts and Procedures* (5th ed.) by Berg, Landreth, and Fall.

Precommitment Stage

Initial Testing of Group Limits

Focus: Superficial and external. It is normal for group members to discuss their external relationships and keep the depth at a surface level. Anxiety is high. Risk, trust, and cohesion are low. Silence is normal.

Important Questions

*   How do I fit into this group?
*   How can I develop trust in the other members and the group process?

Tentative Self-Disclosure

Interaction increases, but group members are still testing the water. Think of this stage as a person getting into the swimming pool. They start off with dipping their toe in but gradually get more and more of their body into the pool.

Healthy norm: self-disclose to belong. Conflict increases: Who is a safe target? Resolved conflict is the gateway to deeper exploration.

Important Question

*   Do I feel a growing sense of belonging in this group?

Leader Role in the Precommitment Stage

- Teach about group process.
- Develop rules and norms.
- Facilitate expression of fears and expectations.
- Model "good" group behavior.
- Provide some structure.
- Assist in formulation of group and individual goals.

Commitment Stage

Depth Self-Exploration

The group will become much more comfortable with a here-and-now focus.
They will begin to see group as a unique place.
Open handling of conflict.
Use group as reality testing lab, begin to establish skill with feedback.

Important Question

- What am I not saying that needs to be said in group?

Commitment to Change

- Focused on doing "work."
- Increased member responsibility for group.

Working Toward Increased Personal Effectiveness

- Members fully capable of helping others.
- Open atmosphere of feedback and sharing.
- Members apply learning to outside.

Preparing to Leave Group

- Link group to external world.
- Discuss the individual meaning of good-bye.

Important Question

- What else needs to be done?

Leader Role in the Commitment Stage

- Continue to model appropriate behavior (especially confrontation).
- Balance support with confrontation.
- Stroke risk-taking.
- Explore common themes.
- Encourage transfer of learning.
- Focus on facilitating, less structure, process observer.

Termination Stage

- Discuss inevitability of end and associated feelings.
- Complete unfinished business with members or leader.
- Teach them how to say good-bye.
- Teach transitioning skills.
- Follow up and evaluation.

Important Questions

- How do I say good-bye to the group and get closure?
- What have I learned from this process?
- What is my next step in the growth process?

The Importance of a Pre-Group Screening Interview

Pre-selection of group members is not always possible. When possible, however, it is the preferred condition. It may be necessary to work in groups with intact populations, for example, or time considerations may interfere with pre-selection procedures. Although a pre-group screening interview is preferred, the group leader will not always be able to afford this luxury, so he or she should sharpen assessment skills and implement procedures to screen during the initial group meeting. The following is a list of essential tasks that should be accomplished either in a pre-group interview or during the initial meeting:

1. **Assess the potential member's readiness for a group experience.** The potential group member should have good motivation for change and an expectation of success.
2. **Select as group members persons who are maintaining at least one minimal primary interpersonal relationship.** This reservoir of successful experience will aid the group member in dealing with the impact of multiple relationships in the group.
3. **Select only persons who have relative absence of pathology or problems too extreme for group members to deal with.** This factor, combined with No. 2, would indicate the need for a referral to individual therapy until such time as the potential member could profit from a group experience. Even in cases where the group is specific to the treatment of certain diagnoses (i.e. groups that focus on major depression or schizophrenia), the members will benefit the most from group through a team-based approach that includes individual, group, and family therapies combined with psychiatric assessments and medication maintenance. Specifically, personality disorders, which represent extreme symptoms that are manifested within relationships, are commonly screened out of groups that are not focused on that specific symptom cluster.
4. **Determine the potential member's "fit" in the group.** Ideally, the total group would be fairly heterogeneous in terms of personality dynamics. This will allow for greater creativity in problem-solving and provide a wider range of interactional possibilities. This is especially important when groups are organized around common problems such as traffic violations, alcoholism, divorce, spousal abuse, or substance abuse.

Pre-Group Interview
Purpose Overview

- Explain the principles of group.
- Describe appropriate behavior.
- Establish importance of attendance.
- Raise expectations about usefulness of group.
- Predict early problems and minimize impact.
- Regular fifty-minute intake.
- Discuss personal goals and how they fit with group (or not).
- Orient to time, location, composition, and goals.
- Describe typical group session.
- Discuss and sign group rules.
- If an open group, discuss recent events/issues.

Segment 1

First Group

Introduction

This segment represents a typical first session. Every group must begin, so every group you facilitate will require you to develop a way to get the group started. It is logical to assume that every group will begin in the first phase of the precommitment stage of development. This means that your group will likely be anxious and will be wondering if this group is right for them. They will be hesitant to share deep, meaningful aspects of self because an atmosphere of trust and safety has not yet formed. Your task as group leader is to welcome them to the group, to orient them to the process, and to get the ball rolling. Respect the group's nervousness and do not try to push them too deep, too fast. Take your time and help them find some commonalities and their own reason for being in the group.

When people get together in groups, most of the people are most afraid of being different and thus, being excluded from the process. Due to this fear, the group will attempt to connect in any way possible. This general group dynamic is known as identification. Think about hanging out at the Student Union coffee shop. A person who is interested in you comes up to your table to try to spark some conversation. What topics will they bring up? If you answered, "Anything to do with college," ("What's your major?" "Studying for exams?"), then you are on target. They will ask that because the question has a high probability of connection. Identification is a wonderful dynamic for group leaders to be aware of because your group will naturally connect if you give them space to do it. It is important to note that the topics will likely be superficial, but that is normal. The beginning points of identification will lay the foundation for deeper connection later on in the group.

Preview Reflection Questions

- Discuss some of your expectations of the first group session. How will group members be feeling? How will you feel as a group leader?

_____

_____

_____

- How would you open the session? How would you close the session?

_____

_____

_____

- What is your role as group leader in the first session? What skills will you use to facilitate the group?

_____

_____

_____

Verbatim

DR. FALL: Good morning everybody and welcome to our first group. The whole purpose of the first group is to spend some time getting to know each other and figuring out what it is we want to get out of group and why we are in the room so we can prepare for our future meetings together. So in that spirit, what I would like to do is spend some time going around and I would like you to say your name and talk a little about what you would like to get out of group and why you are here. Who would like to start?

What is your impression of this opening? How would you open differently?

AMANDA: I'll start. I haven't been in group before but I have been in counseling. I'm at a stage in life where I am trying to find the balance between stepping into professional roles, leaving graduate school, and balancing that with who I always thought I was. I'm struggling with how to navigate and blend those two: who I need to be in work and who I feel I really am.

DR. FALL: I really like that word "balance." You are trying to find balance in your life but it is becoming difficult because you are moving into a transition. So this is a great time to explore that because you are actually experiencing that lack of balance as you make that transition. So I think that would be an excellent thing to try and coordinate here in this group. Thank you, Amanda. Who's next?

Here, Dr. Fall responds to the first group member by validating and summarizing the member statement. He also reflects the word "balance." Finding balance is a universal theme that often appears in group, and he is hoping that this might be something the other group members can relate to, thus increasing the feeling of universality. He also notes that the stated issue is something that can be worked on as the group continues the work. This moves the session along so it is less likely to turn into individual counseling in a group setting.

KURT: Hi, my name is Kurt. I was married for a while and recently we got divorced. I found out she was seeing someone else and since that point, I have been having problems building trust in relationships and trusting others in general. I guess what I wanted out of group was to see what a trusting relationship looks like, how people relate and maybe take something from that and use it in my life.

DR. FALL: So you have experienced a painful transition. It's a little bit different than what Amanda is going through but the same desire to regain a sense of balance. You say you want to work on trust issues in group. You are now in a room of strangers so I would guess that would produce a bit of anxiety for you.

KURT: Yes it does. I was hoping to see where this goes and hoping to meet some people here in group and learn to trust.

DR. FALL: I appreciate your desire to reach out even though you are experiencing that pain from being betrayed and hurt. I think a lot of people would have a tendency to withdraw so I think this group is a courageous first step for you.

KURT: I am looking forward to it.

Kurt's issue is different from Amanda's, but Dr. Fall attempts to link the two issues under the theme of "transitions." He also reflects the issues of trust and mentions the group situation as possibly anxiety-provoking. Once Kurt responds, Dr. Fall provides encouragement and frames Kurt's group attendance as a healthy choice.

At this point, two members have shared. What would you have done different at this stage?

CHALI: I guess I'll go next. My name is Chali, and I have been in groups before and I really enjoyed the experience and learned a lot about myself. I was able to work on different skills interpersonally. I think continuing that self-awareness and learning more about myself and getting to know how I interact with people is what I am looking to get out of group.

DR. FALL: You are looking for that sense of self-exploration. As you listened to Amanda and Kurt, was there anything there that you could relate to?

I (KAF) have to admit I was a little lost with Chali's statement. I was having a difficult time connecting her to the others, so I relied on the tools that are always available to every group leader: reflection and clarification. The reflection conveys understanding, while the clarification question has the greatest probability for getting the information required. In other words, instead of guessing on the link, why not just ask the group member? What would be another way to respond to Chali's information?

CHALI: I think with what Amanda was saying about balancing different parts of her life. That's something I deal with too. I have a professional identity and an identity with my family and friends. You have different roles with them and it's balancing these roles that can be difficult. I related to that.

DR. FALL: That's an important part of the group process. In our pre-group interviews, I learned about each person's therapy experiences, and many of you have had individual counseling. One of the ways group counseling is different is finding those connections. Learning about yourself, which is your stated goal coming in, but you can actually do that by listening to others. I think you just demonstrated that. Great! Thank you, Chali.

Chali does a nice job connecting herself to Amanda. Dr. Fall makes a process observation about the importance of connecting to others in the group and that learning while listening is an important part of group counseling. This helps teach the members about group and gets them to see the work they are doing as a multifaceted process.

Also, notice that Dr. Fall is repeating the name of the person sharing as a transition to the next person. Saying a person's name helps with the group getting to know one another and also helps each member feel like they matter. There is something personal about remembering someone's name.

CAROLINE: I'll go next. My name is Caroline. This is my first time in counseling. I'm nervous. I am here because I have a lot of stress recently. A whole lot on my plate and a whole lot going on. I am trying to figure out how to handle that well and it feels so overwhelming at this point. That is why I am here.

DR. FALL: I saw a lot of head nods as she was talking about that stress. What are some areas of your life that are most stressful for you?

Dr. Fall makes a process observation that notes the nonverbal connection that other members are making to Caroline. This helps members become aware of how they link with one another even when they are not talking or actively working on their own issue.

CAROLINE: It's not necessarily any one thing. It's just that there are a lot of things and a lot of expectations. I am going to school full-time, working two jobs, in a serious relationship, trying to maintain friendships, spend time with my family, about to start a new career, finish up graduate school, and a job search. It's just a lot things that I could handle one at a time, but all at once is just ugh!

DR. FALL: Just that "ugh." You said, "ugh!" That stress release. It sounds like you are stretched really thin.

CAROLINE: Oh yeah! Unbelievably thin.

DR. FALL: Anyone relate to that?

GROUP: [*All laugh and nod.*]

DR. FALL: My guess is that when Amanda was talking about balance, trying to spin all those plates and feeling like you can't add one more . . .

Here, Dr. Fall chose to link Caroline with Amanda on the topic of balance. The group as a whole was responding to the theme so he could have gone with a wider group connection. If you were the group leader, how would you have facilitated a broader group response?

CAROLINE: I almost don't like that word because it gives me something else to stress out about because I know I am not balanced.
DR. FALL: So you are very aware of that.
CAROLINE: Oh yeah.
DR. FALL: Well, good. I think that is something that you share with your group colleagues and is definitely something we can work on as we move forward. Thanks, Caroline.
MALLORY: I'm Mallory. I am in college and studying to be a teacher. I am substitute teaching and recently got married, and it has been hard with time management, trying to figure out how much time I have to complete everything I need for school and work. I stopped working out because I feel I don't have the time, and now that I'm not exercising I feel even more stressed out. I thought by joining a group I could see how other people handle the areas of their life.
DR. FALL: So again that sense of juggling.

This reflection attempts to connect Mallory to the developing theme of struggle with balance.

MALLORY: Yes. I don't feel like I have the time to do everything that I need to get done, so aspects of my life have completely changed, and I don't know how to handle it, like with exercising. I feel like I don't have time for that and I'm constantly stressed by school and work.
DR. FALL: That's a bit of a different aspect then what I've heard from the others, but maybe they share that concern as well. It seems like you have a lot of things to do and the things that get sacrificed are the things that are about you; the self-care types of things.

Dr. Fall attends to the subtle change in the theme and alludes that others might share the issue. The shift detected in Mallory's sharing is that when she struggles with balance, the roles and activities that revolve around her self-care are the things that are the first to be abandoned. This is a potentially very important and personal aspect of the emerging theme.

MALLORY: Yes, and so I get even more stressed out.
DR. FALL: So group can be a place for you to explore that and find out how you can move those types of things more to the forefront.
MALLORY: Yes.
DR. FALL: Is that the case with the people that have gone? Do you find that taking care of yourself either takes a backseat or do you feel fairly balanced and are pretty good about making yourself a priority? How does that fit for you?

This moves the new concept into the group for consideration. I (KAF) wish I would have phrased it in a more open way. I don't like that the first two questions are closed-ended questions. How would you craft a more open-ended response?

GROUP: [*Laughing.*]
CAROLINE: It doesn't fit!
DR. FALL: Am I stressing you out by mentioning that? [*Laughs.*]

It is important to note that the use of humor can be a vital element in group and can be a catalyst for intimacy. It can also be a way to keep the discussion superficial. What is your reaction to the laughter and joking occurring here?

CAROLINE: [*Laughing.*] I am a very neat and organized person, but my apartment is just such a wreck. Whenever I get stressed out, I just don't have time to deal with it even though know I feel so much better, more at peace, when I don't come home with my stuff everywhere. I definitely get where you are coming from.
MALLORY: It's good to hear someone else say that because so many times I feel like I am the only one. I am the only one trying to balance all of this stuff in my life. Like, why me?

Caroline responds to the shift in the group theme and connects with Mallory. Mallory's response to Caroline solidifies the connection (with no help from the leader) and speaks to the curative factor of universality: not feeling alone in one's problems. From a leader's perspective, it is evidence that the group is beginning to relate to one another effectively.

CHALI: A couple of months ago, I went to this training and they were talking about taking care of yourself and I was at a time in my life where I was saying, "You cannot tell me that right now." I am just managing to get by. I can only concentrate on two things in my life, and everything else is falling by the wayside. And you know it's really bad, but I can't do anything about it. It feels difficult when people are saying, "You should be doing this," but they don't understand, I can't.
DR. FALL: Not enough time . . . too overwhelmed. How about for you Kurt? How does that fit in with what you are working on . . . putting yourself first?

The reflection follows Chali's statement and is meant not only for Chali but for every member connected with the theme (Amanda, Mallory, Chali, and Caroline). I (KAF) am aware that Kurt is the only one who has not been involved in the discussion much, so the question to him was designed to gather him to the theme and help him stay with the group. I was also aware that Greg had not shared yet and was worried that he may feel left out. What would you have done in this situation?

KURT: After what I have gone through, I wasn't finding a lot of time to put myself first. I was dealing with too many issues at the same time. I was dealing with a lot of stress like these people too, but it would stem from a different thing. Right now, I am trying to get my things together, trying to build relationships, which I am having problems with, but it goes back to the trust thing. It's the stress of what I have gone through, and it has hurt my relationships. I am trying to get that back together right now.

DR. FALL: I think the attempt to connect is a recognition and a demonstration of you putting yourself out there and first, which is a good thing. I'll throw this out there and perhaps we are not yet connected enough to experience it yet, but coming to group and participating in group is an example of "you time." You carving out this hour and a half to come in, talk about what is important to you, listening to other people, is a great example of putting yourself first. One of the things we are going to have to watch is that you take the time to get your stuff out there. That you don't think, "Oh, I have all these other people to help and their issues are more important," so that each of us take that challenge to carve out some time, to not only see this as "me time," but also take some time in here to get your voice heard. [*Looks at Greg.*] How about you?

Kurt's response allows Dr. Fall to bring him into the developing theme and also opens the door for a process observation that frames group attendance and participation as a way to address the group's issue of taking time for themselves. As a group leader, you want to look for openings to link "good" group behavior with individual goals. This will strengthen the group's attention on the importance of group and will make group instantly integral to what each person wants to get out of the process.

GREG: My name is Greg. I'm a rookie at this. It's my first time in counseling. I heard about this and thought I'd take a chance to come because I want to get a dialogue going about, well, it feels funny talking about this, but about being a Black man in a White world, just navigating that. It's a heightened awareness of difference. I thought about this a lot in terms of coming to a group like this. I would like to learn more about that and be able to vent a little about that. That's where I am at.

DR. FALL: So a part of that experience is feeling different, feeling outside.

GREG: Yeah, very much feeling different. I heard something earlier that resonated with me but from a different aspect when you were talking about roles. I feel that I am often balancing different roles as I interact. The roles aren't professional or personal . . . well, they are very personal. They are how you interact in mixed racial company. They are how you interact in common racial company. It's kind of a weird thing. That's where I'm at.

DR. FALL: My sense is what you want to do here, listening to you, is you want to start a dialogue. You want to start a conversation.

Greg brings up a very important issue. I (KAF) was very aware of time and the fact that Greg chose to go last. At times, members will bring up issues at the end of group because they have some awareness that the subject is "heavy" and the boundary of the end of the session creates a level of safety. Almost like, "I am going to throw this out there, but I know we won't have time to go too deep." At the beginning stages of group, it's also important to not go deep too soon. Trust and safety have not been established to create the atmosphere for processing intense topics. Dr. Fall's response puts the focus on the future and captures the goal as a relational dialogue.

GREG: Yeah.

DR. FALL: If you start that conversation, what are you hoping to learn or gain from that? What is the best outcome?

As I reviewed this response, I was a little worried that this came across as judgmental. Like I was asking him, "What do you really hope to achieve here?" What I was trying to do was get Greg to think about his expectations for the group and to make himself and the group aware of those expectations. My hope was that the awareness would produce a sense of optimism about the topic and the group's role in the process. How would you have responded to Greg at this point in the group?

GREG: A couple of things kind of hit me. One, the value of being able to express some of what I feel. That's a big outcome. From that, being able to learn from that expression. Being able to learn about the whole dynamic. So, that's what hits me when you ask me that question.

DR. FALL: That makes a lot of sense.

GREG: Yeah, it's something personal. I just threw it out there. Like I said, it's my first time dealing with any kind of counseling thing.

DR. FALL: I appreciate the risk you are willing to take and willingness to use this group as a place to establish this dialogue. I am also aware that we don't know each other yet so this might not feel like a real safe place. It is the commitment of the group. Really, to work on any issue requires a risk. It requires each person to try to make this a safe place. Your part of the contract is to get out there too, to be able to state and contribute to the safety so you can get to that place, so we can get to that place, to have that dialogue. I am looking forward to that.

This interchange puts the issue (and all issues) into the hands of the group. It honors the current state of the group relationship (new and tentative) and provides feedback on how, as a group, the members can deepen the relationship. It ends with a return to Greg and gives him a statement of hope that the dialogue will occur within the group.

GREG: Cool.

DR. FALL: Well, today we came in as strangers. I think we did some really good work today because, as I mentioned, the primary goal wasn't to fix everybody's problems and get everything tied up. We have the rest of the life of the group to explore in a deeper way. The purpose of the group today was to break the ice a little bit, to get out in the water, and start the journey of getting to know one another. So we came in today knowing nothing about each other and to know that we had success will be if you learned something about each person. So I have something that I want you to do as a way to wrap up this first group. Take some time to make eye contact with each member of the group. As you do that, I want you to think about the thing that you now know about them that you didn't know when group began. Take a moment to do that.

This represents the end of the first session, and every group leader must close the session in a way that summarizes the work that has been done and provides a vision of what is to come. In this closing, Dr. Fall wants to highlight the purpose of the first session as a first step in the journey. That first step is a simple one: get to know the people you will be working with for the remainder of the group. Looking into the eyes of each group member and thinking of what has been learned is one way to achieve that goal in a interpersonal way. How would you have closed this session?

Reflection Questions

- What elements of the precommitment stage were apparent in this segment?

_____

_____

_____

- What were some leader skills demonstrated in this segment?

_____

_____

_____

- List some things that happened in group that you expected to happen in the first group.

_____

_____

_____

- List some things that did not happen in group that you expected would happen in the first session. Why do you think they did not occur?

_____

_____

_____

After the first session, it is good for the leader to have a sense of what each member's individual goal (what they want to get out of group) and group goal (how they tie into any existing group theme) is as a way to move into the next group. Consider each group member and explore their individual and group goal.

Greg:
Amanda:
Kurt:
Chali:
Caroline:
Mallory:

Segment 2

Moving from External to Here-and-Now Processing

Introduction

Once the group gets a fairly stable foundation of connection, the leader will try to facilitate a stronger level of work by bringing the interpersonal dynamics that have, up to this point, been discussed through external relationships into the here-and-now relationships within the group. This takes some skill on the part of the leader because people are more comfortable discussing rather than *experiencing* relationships. The here-and-now interaction will feel much more intense and might increase the anxiety in the group, but this is normal. The role of the leader is to help fold the here-and-now interactions into the process until the group gradually develops a comfort, and even thirst, for this type of connection.

In this segment, the leader will attempt to move the discussion to the here and now in a few different ways. In one method, Dr. Fall asks the members to think about the external relationship dynamic being discussed and consider what the same dynamic would look like in group. This technique is effective because good group leaders know that people are in group as they are outside of group. What is interesting is that most group members do not realize this is true, or that the group leader knows it. This question allows group members to gain that level of awareness of their interpersonal selves to begin the here-and-now process of the work.

Preview Reflection Questions

- How would you facilitate movement from external relationships to here-and-now group processing? Use examples with the group members if possible.

  _____

  _____

  _____

- If you were a member of this group, what could the group leader do to make you feel more comfortable and safe?

  _____

  _____

  _____

- What role does culture play in this developing group? What aspects of the social-justice model found in Chapter 2 of _Group Counseling_ (5th ed.) are relevant in this experience?

  _____

  _____

  _____

Verbatim

CAROLINE: I have something that I really wanted to talk about today. Last time I mentioned that I really struggle with a lot of stress, and it got really bad this week with things piling up. I did what I always do. I just freeze and feel so paralyzed when everything builds up. It's like I can't do anything about it. I can't do anything to help me get out of that stress, and it makes it build up more and more and more. All I feel I can do is sit on my couch and do nothing. Then, since I feel so stuck, of course I feel guilty because I didn't get all this stuff done. When I try to get it done, the perfectionist in me is like, "Now you just have a couple of hours to get it done so you are never going to get it done like you want to." It just spirals, and I so struggled with that this week.

Caroline begins this group with an issue that plagued her over the week. The theme of stress and balance is prevalent in her story. This is a good example of an "external" issue: an issue that the member reports that is impacting relationships outside of group. The job of the leader is to find a way to fold the external issue into here-and-now group processing. How would you integrate this issue into the present work of the group?

DR. FALL: You have the issue of stress and you are giving us an indication of what you do with that stress and what it does to you. It paralyzes you and gives you that stuck feeling.

CAROLINE: Yeah. Yeah.

DR. FALL: [*Looking at group.*] I noticed you really related to that. Would you like to talk about that a little bit to Caroline?

Dr. Fall acknowledges the nonverbal communication of the group and uses it as an opportunity to invite the group to provide feedback and connect with Caroline. Notice the shift in language used in the first session, "Can anyone relate to that?" which tends to promote sharing about how the member relates in an external relationship capacity ("I do that at work") to asking the group to relate and then "talk to Caroline" about the relation, which promotes here-and-now processing.

MALLORY: I kind of feel like she does, but I don't really get stuck or paralyzed. I feel like I will go home and start working on a lot of homework for school or think about work stuff and I can't really focus on one thing at one time. I'll be doing one thing but I'm thinking about another thing so I'm not really being productive and really, in the long run, getting anything done.

DR. FALL: And that feels a little bit like a stuck feeling because you are so scattered.

MALLORY: Yeah, I guess it does.

DR. FALL: [*Looking around the room.*] Other ways you relate to that?

AMANDA: I was in that stage about two years ago, when everything was just too much. There was nothing I could stop because if I stopped anything it would just make everything else harder. I could even tell in the cadence of my voice that it matches that, and that's not really how I talk anymore so . . . I don't want to give advice, but I have identified with that in the past, and for me, what I experienced was that when I was doing that I was trying to get a lot done but I ended up not being good at anything I was doing because it was just too much. It was a hard season of cutting things out, but I was really afraid to stop doing anything because it didn't seem like there was anything to cut out, but I just did, and then, it's not like it solved the problem, but there was so much peace with doing fewer things that it made it feel like I was actually good at what I was doing.

CAROLINE: But everything feels so crucial! I mean, I work to pay for school, and work to pay the bills, so that is a nonnegotiable. School is kind of a nonnegotiable. I need to graduate so I can get a job in my field. What am I going to say? "OK, Boyfriend, sorry I can't see you for a week," when he is a huge source of support in my life? It just feels like absolutely nothing can give. So I don't know what I can take out to give myself some space. Just feel stuck!

DR. FALL: Really difficult to prioritize and choose.

CAROLINE: Yeah! When everything feels so important.

This is good interaction at this stage of the group. Many members are connecting via a common theme and are beginning to clarify it in various ways. The earlier note about trying to move it to here-and-now processing has had mixed results. The group is still weaving external examples into their sharing, but on the other hand they are feeding off one another's information and responding in a relational manner. What would you do at this point? Would you keep the group flowing as is or try to facilitate more here-and-now interaction? Why?

DR. FALL: That is tough. One of the things that I think about when I am listening to you is how that dynamic is going to look in group. When I was listening to you, one of the things that I heard you say is that when you have a hard time choosing and things start to build up and you start to feel overwhelmed, you become paralyzed. What I am thinking about through my filter, "What does that look like in group?" I'm wondering if there is going to come a time when you feel so overwhelmed that you may choose to just stay on your couch and not come to group?

CAROLINE: Yeah, I will say the thought definitely crossed my mind.

DR. FALL: Because this does just represent another plate in your plate-spinning competition.

CAROLINE: Yeah.

The "What does this look like in group?" analysis of external behavior is an example of how you can start getting your group to focus more on group interaction. Group members behave in group as they do outside of group, so flipping the focus from one to the other is not illogical. So if a member is discussing how she gets aggressive in relationships when she gets scared, you could ask, "What will that look like in group?" and suddenly you are facilitating here-and-now processing.

DR. FALL: Well, for me, as we have discussed before, being here is really crucial. As a way to foreshadow for you, and each of you can do this as you are struggling with your own issues and becoming aware, you can think about "What is this going to look like in group" and see that as a way to work on that issue. So it will be vital for you, when you feel that paralysis, that this will be an opportunity for growth. To come in here and instead of acting out the paralysis and becoming more stressed, that you fight that and do something different by coming in here and talk[ing] about it. [*Group head nodding.*]

CAROLINE: OK.

MALLORY: I kind of felt the same way when I was getting ready to come to group. I saw all of the laundry piled up by the door as I was walking out, and I thought, "Oh, I can stay here and get all of laundry done instead of coming to group."

DR. FALL: I see some head nods. We talked a lot about stress, prioritizing and doing those types of things. So, why come to group? What made you look past the laundry and say, "I'm going to come today"?

MALLORY: Once again, I felt like I was the only one that has laundry to do and homework and dishes and spend time with my husband and focus on work. I knew that there were other people in the group feeling the same way so I could get rid of that feeling if I came to group.

CHALI: An issue that I have been having is that my roommates do not understand that I have all of these things going on and I can't get my laundry done and I can't get everything done that they want done at a certain time, and I just feel like I'm letting everyone else down in my life. It's really difficult because I feel I can't please everyone. I'm letting everyone else down, and there are a million things that need to be done but I can't get around to all of them and I'm just doing the most important things. I'm like, "I'll get to that later." It gets hard to want to do something else extra.

DR. FALL: It sounds like for you, you are prioritizing, but then you feel guilty to not be able to attend to everything, not being able to attend to everyone.

CHALI: Yeah. I feel guilty about the prioritizing. What makes this so important? I have to pay for school and my living expenses. I feel like that is very important. I am paying for this schooling so I need to actually do it so I have to actually do my homework. I'm like, "I told my friend I would email her this" or "I told my roommate I would take care of this," and I feel guilty all the time. Maybe they don't feel that way, but I feel that way because I feel like I'm letting them down. I think I experience that. I will hear their little quips behind my back or they'll say, "Don't ask her to do that," or "I just did it for you because I knew you were really busy," but what I'll hear is, "It's because I knew you couldn't get it done." So, it's frustrating.

DR. FALL: How about the analysis where you think about what that is going to look like in group? How do you think that is going to appear in group?

CHALI: I guess that I will feel I need to attend to all of these people and I will feel guilty for not helping them or that I'm focusing too much on one person or on myself, spending too much time in the group on myself and feeling guilty, like "Gosh, I should be doing something else." Something like that maybe.

At this point, the group seems uneasy about the here-and-now processing, and you can feel them shifting back to external processing. The leader is patient and continues to reflect, validate, and return to the "What does this look like in group?" technique. The pattern continues of helping members see their external issues through the group filter. This continues to help each member reflect on group behavior.

DR. FALL: So it sounds like you will really be up in your head, and that is one impact it might have on the group. Instead of just experiencing the group and relating to other people, you are actually processing and trying to prioritize and second-guessing yourself.

CHALI: And maybe even second-guessing what someone says to me, because I'm like, "What is the meaning behind that? Did they really mean what they just said?" I'm just trying to filter what it means whenever someone says anything. It's kind of hard.

DR. FALL: Anyone else have that experience of anxiety about group now that we are getting to know each other and getting a little deeper, that you find yourself getting up in your head and doing the same type of mental calculation that Chali talked about? What's going on inside your head as we are processing?

GREG: I am still a little nervous in my head as I think about interactions. Still aware of the risk-taking aspect of my journey. I guess from what I have heard, the thing that resonates with me is the second-guessing that I heard Chali talk about. I can relate to some of that. Wow! For what it's worth, being stuck, and that is the word that you used, just tugged at me to hear that. Just that word, how you said it, really tugged at me. Those are some of the things . . .

Notice how this conversation has evolved, and, as it does, subtle elements of the interpersonal issues are uncovered and other members begin a deeper level of relating. We have now identified an initial theme of being stuck and paralyzed, discussed what those issues might manifest in group, and then progressed to the idea of "second-guessing" oneself and others, which can impact relationships in a profound way.

Greg communicates with Chali about her use of the word "stuck." That is a word that has been mentioned before in group, but it stood out for him this time. What do you think this meant to him?

DR. FALL: Yeah, the second-guessing, the feeling of anxiety about connecting and what these relationships mean. Kurt, I know initially you had talked about trust, and that is definitely a core issue of what we are talking about here.

KURT: It sure is. I'll admit I'm a little anxious with some of the dialogue between people right now. I'm not really sure how to make a relationship work in group yet. Maybe through some dialogue, and, as I get comfortable, I'll be able to form some rapport with some of the group members here. We'll go from there.

DR. FALL: Not to sound too "counselor-ly," but this is exactly where we need to be. Wouldn't it be unreal if, in the beginning of group, once we go through our names suddenly we just trust everybody and we are able to get real automatically? I think what we are struggling with, whether it is stress from priorities or others, at the core it is really about relationships and making those decisions and what that does to us. That all develops, and what we are doing is developing. So where we are now is completely normal. Feeling a little bit anxious, but feeling a little closer. There is a new type of anxiety that comes from getting closer, and that's almost where we are. My encouragement to you is: each one of you is at the stage where you have the desire to connect more, but you are thinking about it a lot. Group can be a great place, a laboratory, to practice getting out there. Experiencing. Doing. Verbalizing what is in your head and let[ting] us work with it. That is how these relationships are going to form. So, as we move forward, I hope there is a sense of comfort in the room that we begin to do that. As things come up in our brains, instead of silencing them we start to get them out a little bit more. How does that sound?

KURT: Sounds good.

Dr. Fall makes a process observation about the status of the group processing designed to normalize the here-and-now focus. As groups begin relating to each other, it is normal for them to feel uneasy or even confused as they wonder why they are not focusing on their external issues. Knowing that deeper learning about self and others will come from the here-and-now processing can give the group a sense of hope that they are doing good and productive work.

AMANDA: It brings up a new anxiety in me. I wasn't anxious until you said that! [*Laughs.*]

DR. FALL: Great! I did my job. [*Laughs.*] It should create a new anxiety because it is a risk. That's really what we are talking about in here: risk. Risk to do something new. Risk to get out there and work instead of keeping it all inside.

CHALI: When you said that, I was thinking of taking a risk and asking Greg what he meant by his second-guessing. I have a perception of my second-guessing, but you said you feel that way too. I don't know . . . just to hear someone else's thoughts on that.

GREG: I guess the way I would answer that is . . . when you said is there any other meaning behind what was said, that kind of resonated with me. I feel that I have been gifted with great antennae. I have great antennae. I know that. I just pick up sometimes the energy of our conversation. What's really going on here? Often, my antennae will pick up something different than what is going on at the surface. Sometimes I'll think maybe that's me, but as I go on, I'll get some other affirming things. It's kind of hard to hide that. Yeah, she's not comfortable, for whatever reason. And you wonder what's up with that? Or he's kind of weird with me and not normal. What's up with that? So that's kind of the second-guessing. For me, it is particularly an interracial thing. It gets old after a while, to try to process that stuff.

This is a great example of a group member taking a risk to experience here-and-now interaction. Chali is reaching out to Greg and looking for clarification and connection regarding an element they had in common (second-guessing). It opens the door for Greg to share about his "antennae," which could be useful in later groups as it sheds some light on his interpersonal style.

DR. FALL: Did that answer your question? Help you clarify?

CHALI: Yes.

DR. FALL: You feel like you understand him better. My guess is, and correct me if I'm wrong, we all second-guess to a certain degree, but when you pick up those things, it is not always safe to clarify with that other person, to say, "I'm picking up something a little bit different, can you tell me what is under the surface?"

GREG: Oh wow! For me, not only is it not always safe, but it's irritating because I will not clarify with that other person so it becomes an internal dialogue for me that I have to step through. All of the self-questioning. You wonder, "Am I right? Am I wrong?"

DR. FALL: Lots of questioning. Probably similar to what she said . . .

GREG: Oh yeah!

DR. FALL: Well, I hope as we move forward that group becomes a safe place where you can clarify. Where, as your antennae are picking up those kinds of things in the group, that you are able to say, "Hey, I want to know what's going on with that. Tell me a little bit more" and do that exploration. The worst thing to happen is for you to just replicate what happens on the outside; that it all stays in here [*motioning inside self*]. We are able to say what we are thinking and give language to the unspoken questions we have about relationships in here as we move forward.

Reflection Questions

- What are some ways Dr. Fall attempted to bring the here and now into the discussion? What would you have done differently?

  _____

  _____

  _____

- What are some ways in which the group resisted here-and-now interaction? Why was it happening?

  _____

  _____

  _____

- What is your opinion of using the "What does that look like in group?" filter as a way to bring external interpersonal dynamics into the group?

  _____

  _____

  _____

- Greg uses the metaphor of "antennae." How would you use that in the group to foster here-and-now interaction?

  _____

  _____

  _____

- What are your impressions of the group members and their connection with the group? Who is connected to whom? Who seems the least connected at this point, and what would you do to get them more involved as the group moves forward?

  _____

  _____

  _____

Segment 3

Managing Conflict

Introduction

One of the most difficult issues for group leaders to handle is the appropriate management of conflict. Most people are so scared of conflict that it creates an avoidance response that can facilitate stagnation in the group. Conflict does not have to mean cruel fighting with name calling or other forms of abuse. While conflict does look like that in some relationships, it is not what you want to happen in your group. Both leaders and group members come into group with bad experiences with conflict, so it is possible for the entire group to be invested in keeping things "nice."

Unfortunately, relationships need conflict to grow. Disagreement and comfort with differences of opinion, reflect a deepening sense of comfort and safety within the relationship. People feel free to be themselves without the precommitment fear of being rejected and excluded from the group. Despite the need for conflict, people are still anxious about it. It is out of this anxiety and need that the leader must be vigilant for the growing tension in the group. Group members will often target the leader as the first experience of conflict because the leader is the safest person in the room. In this segment, Dr. Fall decides to make a process observation about the stuck feeling in the group, which provides the catalyst for a confrontation. It is important for group leaders to remember that conflict has the potential to be a growth catapult for the group, not to avoid it but to embrace it by first validating the speaker and then making sure to respond openly and nondefensively. Skillful resolution of conflict will be the golden door to serious work within your group.

Preview Reflection Questions

- What has been your own experience with conflict in relationships? What does the conflict look like to you?

  _____

  _____

  _____

- What are your feelings about managing conflict in group?

  _____

  _____

  _____

- What are some leadership skills that are important to appropriately managing conflict in the group?

  _____

  _____

  _____

- Based on your knowledge of this group, where might conflict arise?

  _____

  _____

  _____

Verbatim

DR. FALL: Welcome back everybody. This is the fifth group session we have had, and we have made a lot of progress. Before we start with our usual getting into it that we've been doing for the past couple of weeks, I just wanted to bring something up. I was reflecting on the work that we've done, and I think that we, as a group, have progressed quite a bit from the first time that we met. We are starting to identify some themes and really start[ing] to work with one another, addressing that desire for connection and fear of connection at the same time. I think that relates to everyone's individual goals, and it's become somewhat of a group goal. As I was reflecting, I couldn't help but sense a sense of being stuck. I don't know if that is a reflection of what we have been talking about. Many of you have said that when you get overwhelmed you get to that stuck place. I am sure that has a bit to do with it. I am also thinking it has something to do with where we are going as a group. I don't really know how to fix that or if I need to say anything more than that, but I just wanted to express that and throw it out to the group to see if you had any feedback about the group "stuckness."

This is an example of the leader initiating and inviting conflict within the group. Here, the leader has indicated that upon reflection he notices both progress and a nagging feeling of being stuck. Notice how he doesn't attempt to be the expert and name or blame the group for the stagnation. This is one way to begin the process of conflict from a non-defensive and non-attacking stance. I (KAF) was a bit nervous when offering this to the group, and I think that was evident in the length of the statement. On the other hand, it did convey a sense of concern and tentativeness that could be seen as appropriate for the group's first experience with potential conflict. How would you have offered up the leader's awareness and the processing of it differently?

MALLORY: I kind of feel stuck because I am still so stressed out at home and with my roles now, being a college student, and work and wife, I just feel my husband does not understand. I kind of feel that you, as a male counselor, do not understand the roles of a wife. I go to school at night and get home late, and then there are dishes to do, there's laundry to do, and I just feel I have to do all of it. I kind of feel you don't understand that just being a male, and my relationship with male and female roles.

Mallory takes the first risk here. Notice her tentative language: multiple uses of "kind of," which softens the impact of her confrontation. It is important for the leader to acknowledge Mallory's concern, without becoming defensive. What would you say to Mallory?

DR. FALL: So you are experiencing that in your own relationship and you are also experiencing that with me?

Critique Dr. Fall's response on the elements of acknowledgment and nondefensiveness.

MALLORY: Right. I just kind of feel you don't understand all of the roles I have to take on. It's getting hard trying to convey to you all I need to balance and trying to balance all of the roles where I don't feel so stuck and stressed.

DR. FALL: Yeah, and I sense that there is something even deeper there. It's not just about understanding all of the different things you have to do but also what that means to you as a person, as a woman, with all those things to do.

MALLORY: Right. I feel like I should be the one who does all the dishes, the laundry, and cleans the house, because I do feel that is the wife's role, but then I feel like maybe my husband is telling me he'll do it. Kind of like what Chali was saying. I hear him say he'll do it, and he'll do it, but he's saying it maybe because I can't do it. So then I feel like he doesn't understand the roles of the wife. With just being a male, I feel like there are so many more pressures on women on balancing so many roles and sometimes I feel like you will never be able to understand.

It's interesting, and common, that Mallory took the issue back into the external relationship and away from the leader. This could be an indication of discomfort. It is great that she brought to back to the here and now at the end of her sharing. If she had not, it would have been good for the leader to facilitate movement back to the present interaction.

DR. FALL: So there is a difference between us that you are concerned about. You are really wanting me to get that and are concerned that I am not.

MALLORY: Yeah.

GREG: Yeah, I feel the same thing, with all candor. I really do. I really do. Even when you talked just now. You talked about the things we have talked about, feeling overwhelmed, etc. I haven't talked about that. I have been talking about feeling different, and you didn't even acknowledge that. I feel a little uncomfortable being so animated, but that's just what hit me as I heard you talk. Since you asked, I sometimes feel that you are hearing me, but sometimes I feel that you hear them a lot better than you hear me. I really do. So you asked, and now you know.

Greg links in with Mallory's theme of being misunderstood by the leader. It is somewhat uncommon for a confrontation "chain" to form the first time the group experiences conflict, mainly because most groups will rally to regain homeostasis after the first taste. Usually, the leader needs to hold the group within the conflict so it can be resolved without avoiding it. In this group, the leader will not only need to attend to the two vocal members (Mallory and Greg) but must also be aware of how the intensity is impacting the rest of the group. How would you respond at this point?

DR. FALL: I did. First, I appreciate that you said that because one of the things that we specifically talked about was that you had those "antennae." My guess is that you were picking up something under the surface with me and you've been doing a lot of thinking about it, and one of the things we talked about is you taking the risk to clarify and wonder what was going on.

Critique Dr. Fall's initial response to Greg on the elements of acknowledgment and non-defensiveness.

GREG: I appreciate you saying that.

DR. FALL: Saying something is the start of that dialogue. What I heard you say is that it is very important for you that I and the rest of the group know that it is very painful for you to feel different.

GREG: Yeah, it is. It's uncomfortable. Even more important, I was sharing with you that it's irritating to feel ignored. It's irritating to feel ignored. I'm not stupid. Maybe some of that is me. Maybe some of that is me, but you talked about throwing that stuff out into the group and that's what I felt. Maybe that is why I am a little stuck.

This is a great example of what happens when the leader does not reflect the most important aspect of the member's statement. The leader missed the part of feeling ignored. The good thing is that the member was able to highlight this aspect and stay engaged with the relationship. This is a good sign and is a common outcome when the leader can maintain the atmosphere of safety within the conflict. The member is more likely, even in a moment of disconnection, to feel comfortable enough to stay with it rather than check out.

DR. FALL: That makes sense to me. Not feeling that someone understands you, not feeling like you are being heard, can lead people to not wanting to take the next step or the risk. As we discussed, it doesn't feel safe. If I don't get where you are coming from, if I don't understand, at a very core level, then it is not going to feel safe to take the next step.

GREG: Right! Yeah . . . yeah.

Here Dr. Fall attempts to connect both Greg and Mallory and summarize the issue. What do you think of where the group is at the moment? What would you do next?

DR. FALL: How about other people in the room? That's what I was . . . I think that's what I was feeling, that stuckness, wanting to take that next step, which is a greater risk. Other people's feeling about that?

AMANDA: I wanted to respond to what Greg said, because I haven't disclosed in group, but I am bi-racial, and I have a lot of feelings, not so much in this group, but in everyday life. Feeling that conflict and feeling not understood, not listened to, and so I identify with the same frustration. I came here to work on more of the professional and home–life balance, but I have that similar issue of, "Am I really understood? Am I really heard?" or if I am different is that being blamed on my race? I just think it's even harder if you feel unheard by someone who you expect to hear you like your counselor or your group leader. I just wanted to share in that, and it's a real experience. I know it can hurt even more. When I have gone to someone who I expect will really listen to me and really hear me and I feel they are somewhere else and have their own ideas of what is going on, it's so much more hurtful.

DR. FALL: [to Greg] How was that for you to hear what Amanda had to say?

GREG: I really appreciate hearing that. I didn't know that. I really appreciate hearing that, for what it's worth. I appreciate that. I appreciate that.

The leader had a choice as to what to do with Amanda's input. He could have addressed the individual issue or the connection to Greg. Dr. Fall chose to focus on the connection to Greg. What might be some reasons to go with Amanda's individual issue? What is the rationale for going with the relational issue?

You may have noticed that Dr. Fall has not been working in depth with either Mallory or Greg to resolve their feelings. Often, trying to "solve" the problem will result in greater frustration on the part of the member. Think about the concept of feeling misunderstood and ignored. How do you solve that in a group? Do you try to demonstrate that you do understand what it means to be a woman or an African-American man? Doing so would probably come across as demeaning and dismissive. Instead, you can convey understanding and attention by providing those qualities that convey them in a relational way: listening, reflecting, creating an atmosphere of openness. Dr. Fall wants the members to feel understood and attended to so he is attempting to relate and interact with each of them in those ways.

DR. FALL: [to group] Other thoughts or experiences about taking that next step, feeling stuck, or even what has gone on today with some of the risking that has gone on here?

CAROLINE: Honestly, these conversations just make me so uncomfortable. It makes me want to take several steps back, but then when I really think about it, it's seeing you guys were really taking a big risk talking about that. I don't know, it's kind of anxiety-provoking, but at the same time I really value and respect that fact you can be so open about things that are so personal to your experience. You barely know me and I don't know you that well . . . yeah.

DR. FALL: I think that is one of the things risk feels like. It feels anxiety-provoking. My guess is that as each of you shared today, before you decided to say and disclose that to me, you felt that anxiety inside. Greg, you were relating to what Mallory had to say, the courage that it took to say something, not keep it in your head, but say it out loud, that is what risk feels like.

GREG: There is no doubt about that. It's kind of funny, I was kind of irritated, with all candor, but I feel a little better [smiles], for what it's worth.

The processing is moved to the group-as-a-whole level in order to get everyone involved in the processing. With two confrontations and one connection-oriented disclosure, the atmosphere seems safe for everyone to participate. Caroline's statement about her feelings of anxiety surrounding "these conversations" reflect a feeling that most of the members are probably experiencing. Dr. Fall reframes the confrontations as "risks" and connects the anxiety to the normal process of risk-taking. Greg responds in a positive manner, which lets the leader know he is moving with the flow of the group.

DR. FALL: I'll ask the two of you, and really anybody can chime in because as a group we are all part of the stuck feeling. We are all contributing to it and will contribute to movement in some way. Thinking about that lack of understanding, what is it that you would need from the group, or me, but probably better from the group, to move forward? What would help you increase that feeling of being understood?

This is an attempt to get the group to also consider the next step of the conflict-management process: to consider what each person would need to move the relationship in a positive direction. It doesn't mean the group is finished processing but gives them an additional layer to integrate.

MALLORY: Well, I think the part about self-care that you mentioned in one of our earlier sessions, just learning how to be more self-aware and take care of self and not worry about the other roles and the balance that goes along with that until you really know yourself and how I am interacting with other people through other relationships.

DR. FALL: So maybe giving your time in group to really share that and explore it would be helpful to you?

MALLORY: Yes, that would really help a lot. Just to be more self-aware, increase my self-awareness, along with self-care, before I try to take on all of these other roles and how people see my roles.

DR. FALL: OK. How about for you, Greg?

GREG: It's funny, that personal risk-taking kind of helped a lot. Feeling that you are not as different as you think you are kind of helped out a lot. That was good, and I'll just leave that at that. That happened in group, knowing that you are heard. See where that goes . . .

KURT: I think it takes a lot of courage to take a risk like some of you have done, and that's a hard thing to do. That's something I am trying to work on too. You know, building some courage up, taking some risks, and hopefully, in return, you will build relationships that way. That's kind of what I am thinking right now.

DR. FALL: For me, going along with what Kurt said, is that we have to be willing to take that risk to get the payoff we are looking for in our relationships.

GREG: I hear you.

Both Mallory and Greg mention the impact the sharing had on each of them. Mallory gains some insight into how it connects with her individual goal. Kurt does a nice job of framing the risk as "courageous," which certainly puts a positive spin on the type of sharing done within the group. He also mentions how it is connected to his goal.

DR. FALL: I think that is really what we did today. When you are looking for understanding, and you are concerned and afraid that you are not being understood, there is no way we are going to wrap it up, nothing I can say that will make you go, "Oh, he gets me now" or "That man knows what it's like to be a woman." There's nothing I can say. But what I think we have done as a group today is acknowledge the risk that it took, that is an important part of understanding. I know that I am committed to being willing to be open to learn and to share in that dialogue you are looking for. I think at the end of the journey we will be closer to understanding than we were before. Is that something that, as a group, feels good? A commitment to a willingness to go together into that next step?

GROUP: [Nods.]

The leader makes sure that the group is not expecting the issues to be completely resolved and that they are seen as a process that will develop as the relationships develop. The goal at this point is to get comfortable with "being real," followed by all parties committing to stay engaged in the group relationships while being honest, so growth can occur.

CHALI: It's kind of scary to be that open with people. You guys were really brave today and I'm proud of you guys because you were the first ones to step out and say something, like models for the rest of us.

MALLORY: Well, thank you for saying that because it makes me feel a lot better because I do have trouble taking risks and letting people know how I feel. I think that's how I got in this stuck position in the first place.

DR. FALL: Good. So, moving forward, this is something we can build on. We had quite a few members jump in and take that plunge, test the waters, and everything is not rainbows and flowers. We are still people struggling to understand one another, but hopefully that struggle looks safer than it did before. OK, I will see you next week.

Reflection Questions

- How did this session meet and not meet your expectations for conflict management?

  _____

  _____

  _____

- One of the most difficult aspects of managing conflict is balancing individual and group levels of processing. Explore the leadership techniques employed in the segment for each level.

  _____

  _____

  _____

- In this segment, the areas on conflict were race and gender. These elements were distilled and discussed at a relational level (feeling misunderstood and feeling unheard and ignored). What are the costs and benefits of this approach? How would you have done it differently?

  _____

  _____

  _____

- Conflict is often anxiety-provoking. What are some aspects of managing conflict that create the most anxiety for you?

  _____

  _____

  _____

- If you were co-leading this group, how could you use the co-leader relationship to model conflict management?

  _____

  _____

  _____

- As this group becomes more comfortable, where do you see them going? How would you facilitate movement into a deeper commitment stage of development?

  _____

  _____

  _____

Segment 4

Commitment to Working as a Group

Introduction

As the group gets settled in the commitment stage, a number of important dynamics fall into place and build on one another. A good experience with conflict resolution will increase the level of trust in the group, which will, in turn, produce deeper self-disclosure, more appropriate confrontation, and better feedback. The group will begin to feel comfortable with the here-and-now processing and begin a consistent pattern of "doing work." As all of these dynamics come together, the group leader can be confident that the norms support healthy group processing and can adopt the role of the process observer, making sure that the group maintains a consistent movement that produces deeper exploration.

The segment was chosen to demonstrate some ways in which the leader can shift from a more directive leadership style (authoritarian to democratic) to a more laissez-faire approach. While elements of a more directive style are needed in the precommitment stage, in the commitment stage it is appropriate to allow the group to do the work, as it will be fairly capable at this point. Being directive at this stage can produce stagnation in the group, as the leader stifles ownership and the practicing of good interpersonal skills. This shift can create anxiety in the group leader as worry about control typically surfaces for some leaders. As you watch the segment, pay attention to the role and activity of the leader and note the times when and how he chooses to intervene and participate in the group.

Preview Reflection Questions

• As the leader takes on a more process observation role, what would be the most difficult aspect of this role for you?

_____

_____

_____

• What norms have formed in the group so far that would support a smooth transition into this stage of development?

_____

_____

_____

• Based on what you know about the group members, which ones are most likely to be ready for more responsibility within the group process? Why? Which ones might be hesitant? Why?

_____

_____

_____

Verbatim

CHALI: I wanted to start off today asking Kurt how you are doing with the trust issues you said that you had and how that is playing out in group.

Chali begins the session with a direct connection to Kurt. This is typical for this stage in group, as members are ready to get to work and spend less time getting into the flow of the group. Notice her eye contact with Kurt, but also notice that she seems somewhat anxious and tentative. That is also normal until all group members get comfortable with the pace and depth of the processing. From a leader's perspective, Chali might be anxious, but it represents a nice step for her to be willing to connect despite the nervousness.

KURT: OK. Well, as we have kind of been talking about through the weeks I have been having trust issues since my break-up or divorce from my wife. I have noticed these things over the last year. You know, I've tried dating and at some point during the dating process, I'll be sitting there and listening to what my partner has to say and I'll be thinking in the back of my mind, "She doesn't really mean this. She's lying about this. Something is wrong here." That has happened several times. I always think that someone has ulterior motives now and trying to play mind games and the trust isn't there. That has kind of spilled over in my work and business. I'm having deals with my business partners and I have this thing in the back of my mind saying, "This person isn't telling me the truth anymore," or "They are playing a game with me," like I've said about my relationship issues. It's always in the back of my mind that someone is not telling me the truth, and I have a major issue with that, but at the same time I have been trying to work through some of that in group. I have learned some things along the way and I'm hoping it's helping me in my life situations. So that's kind of where I'm at right now.

Kurt responds to Chali's query by disclosing his internal dialogue when he interacts with people. The content is about his external relationships, but what are the process components of his statement?

GREG: It must be a drag always second-guessing yourself in your interacting.

KURT: It is! It is very stressful.

GREG: That's gotta be a drag.

KURT: It is. Just as everything in my life went down, my ability to trust just broke in there. I've been trying to pick up those pieces and go from there.

DR. FALL: How about with what just happened? Chali is a woman and just asked you a very personal question about wondering what is going on with you and I am wondering what went through your mind as you heard her question.

Dr. Fall attempts to focus Kurt on the issue as it is being experienced in group. Following this path, Kurt has an opportunity to work on his trust issue in the here and now.

KURT: Hmm . . . I was glad that she checked in with me.

DR. FALL: Go ahead and talk to her about it.

It is often important at the beginning of the commitment stage to remind group members to speak directly to one another instead of processing through the group leader. This heightens the intensity of the here-and-now interaction.

KURT: OK. I was glad you checked in with me. It made me feel good that someone would ask me about that. Since we have built some rapport here throughout the weeks, actually I feel that I am starting to trust some of you here in group, and Chali, you specifically right now, and that really helps me when you check in with me and ask how I am doing.

CHALI: That's kind of where I was at when I was asking you, that was to let you know that we are all hearing you. We all care about your issue, just like you have given us space to talk about our issues. I'm glad that you are opening up to us and that you feel that you can trust us with some of these things that have been really hard for you.

It is interesting that Chali makes a shift from "I" to "us." What do you think facilitated the shift? What would you do, if anything, with this?

KURT: Thank you. That makes me feel good. I guess another thing is . . . I identify with Greg with some of your issues and how you interact with different races and how you think they perceive you. I would think that you had some trust issues. How are you dealing with those issues if you have those?

GREG: Yeah, I guess I could say that. We have been meeting a while here, and, I have to be up-front, I feel a little more comfortable in terms of talking with everyone here in the group. That feels good. Still get the second-guessing as you talked about that you have to deal with. I guess for me, more than the trust thing, is you get tired of the second-guessing, tired of wondering if there are games being played, that's what resonates with me.

KURT: Off of the second-guessing term you used, I used to be the type of person that trusted everybody. I would always take their word for things. I would always look for the best in people, and now, it seems like I am just looking at the negative parts of things, second-guessing.

GREG: This is from your divorce?

KURT: I think that is where it stemmed from. There was a break somewhere in there and I'm having an issue with that. I am still struggling with it.

What do you make of this interchange? What is Kurt's purpose for connecting with Greg? What do you think of Greg's response?

DR. FALL: My guess is when you do that second-guessing and you perceive that, as you (Greg) mentioned, other people are playing games or being less than upfront with you, that you have a tendency to withdraw and pull back.

KURT: I think that is very accurate. I do.

DR. FALL: I'm wondering how other people have perceived Kurt in group? One of the things he is working on is trust and working past that fear and trying to stay connected. What times have you been aware of when he has either disconnected, felt him withdraw, or times that you felt him really stay in there? So think of something, your experience of him, and share that with him.

Dr. Fall reflected an additional layer of Kurt's trust dynamic: what he does interpersonally when he does not trust. He then attempts to bring the group into the dialogue by asking them to give feedback to Kurt on their experience of him in group, either connecting or disconnecting. Up to this point, they have been discussing issues and using a mix of external and here-and-now interaction. Encouraging direct feedback is an attempt to get the group to stay in the here and now.

AMANDA: I have really felt like impressed. I've never said anything because it's awkward, but you track so well with all of us and you seem to really have insight or comment and even just caring about what is going on because what I feel what I came in to work on is so different from what you came to work on, but you are still here and you are engaging so that has seemed to me to be really impressive. As someone who, you even expressed, that coming in you did not feel super comfortable in the group but you stayed committed to the work. That's been my experience of you.

KURT: OK.

CAROLINE: I think for me, kind of similar, we came in for very different things, and I just can't imagine what you have gone through, what you are currently going through, and I know at the very beginning when you talked about it I was just very intimidated by that. How do my issues of stress compare to your life completely changing? One of my fears from the beginning was that maybe you wouldn't view our problems as a big of a deal as yours, but just the way you have engaged with us you have made me feel that what I am going through is a big deal and that has just meant the world to me.

Both Amanda and Caroline stroke Kurt. This is normal for a group's initial experience with feedback. The group is cohesive enough to handle the intensity of feedback but still anxious about the possible ramifications of being critical. It is interesting that Caroline discusses a fear of judgment or being minimized by Kurt. This represents more complex feedback.

KURT: Kind of in response to that, off the top of my mind, in no way did I feel that anybody's problems were less significant than mine to start out with at all. I think that everyone deals with their problems differently and has different perceptions about those problems. Like, for example, the stress in your life sounds like it has really been affecting you just as my problems have affected me. I don't see it as one less or more than the other. So, thank you for your input.

Kurt does a nice job here responding to Caroline's concern. Note that he does so in a very nondefensive manner. This response can often be attributed to how conflict management is resolved early in the group. (Remember: listen and respond in a nondefensive way.)

CAROLINE: You have no idea how much that means to me to hear.
MALLORY: I like how Caroline said about him perceiving our problems, and I like how you said our problems did matter to you. If I'm sitting here talking about gender roles and trying to balance a relationship with other things that I have going on and you're recently divorced, I kind of felt like me saying that would make you withdraw from the group. I felt it really brought you in to connect all of us to show that even though our problems are so different that we are all still connected.
CHALI: I am just really impressed with all the bravery with everyone sharing, taking risks to share in the group, and you trusted us, even just a little bit. It helps me to understand and do less second-guessing in my personal relationships at home and even here because I feel like you will tell me what you are really meaning. I don't have to second-guess. Whenever I confronted Caroline, or you, Kurt, you would let me know. I need this from the group and you . . . Greg was even saying what he needed from the group. That makes me feel more comfortable.
KURT: One thing I am feeling right now is this dialogue we are having right now, I feel I am closer to you guys just by having these conversations. I think this is helping me, that it is very helpful to become closer with people and talk with them about their problems and my problems. We are both people. So . . . thank you.
DR. FALL: It sounds like the risk isn't as scary as it was before because of the connections you have made. You feel supported in being more of your real self.
GREG: You feel more comfortable. It makes you feel more comfortable when you get to interact with people and you feel a little more accepted. You're right.

DR. FALL: I did want to check in with you because, as Kurt was relating to your issue, he has a similar thing going. He didn't call them antennae, he talked about hearing someone talk and then processing and wondering. I am wondering as Kurt connected with you, what were your antennae saying?

Dr. Fall is connecting the antennae metaphor to here-and-now processing. This provides Greg an opportunity to share openly about what his antennae are saying in the present interaction. This models good open processing and directly addresses the second-guessing line of discussion.

GREG: They were saying . . . that he was real. That he was real and reaching out. [*He turns to look at Kurt during this sentence.*] It felt natural. I think that's a part of us being together for a while and working with each other. It feels a lot more natural, at least from my perspective.

CHALI: I get that naturalness too. That we can bring things up and it's a comfortable place to be. I mean, a little scary, anything you bring up from yourself and share with the world is a little scary, but I feel like you guys are going to listen and give me real feedback.

GREG: I like what you said, but it is more comfortable. I like what you said earlier. I feel that is I throw something out there, I don't feel like I have to second-guess as much what people are saying, and that's kind of a good-news story. Kind of makes me think why I can't translate that more out there in the world. But you are right, it's kind of more comfortable.

CAROLINE: Greg, you have no idea how good it is for me to hear you say that. For me, I have been wondering what your antennae are saying about me. So, hearing you say that this is a place that you feel you don't have to second-guess yourself makes me breathe this huge sigh of relief knowing that I'm not adding to your problem. You know, adding to the thing you want to work on. That's good to hear.

GREG: Thanks, but more thanks to you guys . . . being more trusting.

DR. FALL: It works in so many different ways. I mean, we have done a lot of hard work in checking those things out, whether they are antennae or we call them second-guessing, we all have that mechanism, and you have each done a lot of work getting outside of your head and processing that in the group. You don't have to wait to do that, right? If you are wondering how someone is perceiving you in group, and you are feeling that in the moment, then that is really the next step, to say, "You know, I know this doesn't have anything to do with what we are talking about, but Greg, I'm wondering about us. I'm wondering if there is anything you need to say to me? or if there is anything you have perceived about me because your perception is important." That's the next step. We don't get that a lot in relationships, but if you are feeling in the group that we are beginning to get to a place of honesty and openness, then that is the next step.

Reflection Questions

- What do you think of Dr. Fall's process observation role in this segment? What would you have done differently?

  _____

  _____

  _____

- One fear at this stage is that groups will become too cohesive. Looking back over the segment, how would you describe this group's level of cohesion? What would you do to facilitate a change, if needed?

  _____

  _____

  _____

- In this segment, the group is beginning to experiment with more direct work with one another. List some examples that illustrate this type of work.

  _____

  _____

  _____

- What forms of resistance, if any, do you note in the group so far? What would you do as the leader to address them?

  _____

  _____

  _____

Segment 5

Preparing for Termination

Introduction

At first glance, this topic might seem a little strange for inclusion. Most of the videos and books on group do not spend very much time discussing the importance of preparing a group for termination. However, I have found that preparing for the end of group largely determines the effectiveness of your termination session and thus, the "take-away" experience of the group. Merely reminding the group that termination is approaching does not seem to be enough to capture the wide range of issues that emerge at this stage of group development. It is vital that leaders recognize that a person's history of ending relationships will greatly influence how they perceive and participate in the end of the group relationship. If, given the chance, gaining insight into the interpersonal pattern of ending can provide one last growth opportunity for members. Ignored, the unhealthy good-bye dynamics can result in no-shows, volatile emotions, or a return to pre-group symptomology and complaints.

This segment provides, in a very short amount of time, four elements of the termination preparation. First, you will hear the leader remind the group that termination is coming soon. Next the leader broadens the frame of termination to consider how one's personal experience of good-byes can impact termination. Next, you are given an example of processing unfinished business within the group. Last, you can observe how the leader becomes more active in facilitation again. Even though the group is still working and committed to using here-and-now interaction, the leader recognizes that the group will need some direction as the end nears. As such, the leader's behavior more closely reflects a precommitment mode rather than one of process observation. All four of these are options for you as you consider how to prepare your group for termination.

Preview Reflection Questions

- What do you think "learning to say good-bye" means? Discuss your experience of good-byes in relationships. How do you think these experiences will impact your ability to terminate groups effectively?

_____

_____

_____

- Trust is a theme this group has been working on. What are some ways this theme might interact with the dynamics of termination?

_____

_____

_____

- What would you do, as a leader, to prepare this group for termination?

_____

_____

_____

Verbatim

DR. FALL: Welcome back to group. As we've been talking about the last few weeks, next week is our last group. It will be our last time together. So this will be a time when we start wrapping things up. It will be a chance for us to say good-bye to the group, to the members of the group, and the work that we have done. I know that saying good-bye often brings up some pretty powerful memories, and without processing those, it can actually get in the way of the work that we need to do to say good-bye to each other. We all have a history of good-byes and not all of them have been positive. Some of them have been very painful, so I wanted to give space to talk about that in preparation for the work we will do next week. So what I wanted to do is just provide a space for each one of you to share, when I say "saying good-bye," what comes up for you?

This is an example of opening a session where the goal is to prepare the group for termination. Notice that Dr. Fall mentions "as we have been talking about for the last few weeks." It is very important to gradually expose and illuminate the process of termination so it is not a surprise to your group. With termination coming the following week, Dr. Fall is moving away from the process observer role and is becoming a more active facilitator, much like in the beginning stages of group.

AMANDA: For me, the first thing I think of is the only real good-bye I have had recently, within the last couple of years, [which] was really bad. It was an ending of a relationship that was so severe that we don't have any contact. I have a propensity to want, even if the relationship isn't functional, in one sense I am the one to say, "OK, when we go our separate ways, I still think fondly of you and I'll still care and check in on you once in a while." We totally can't do that. And so I kind of feel group is that same way because we don't know each other outside of group so I'm not going to be able to call Caroline and say, "Hey, I just saw this ad about having too much to do and I thought of you and I wanted to check in." So it feels like that good-bye was really unnatural and I feel it's going to be like that here.

Amanda is relating a good-bye experience that felt "unnatural." Notice how quickly she moves from the external relationship to the group. Even as the leader's behavior shifts to a more active role, which can feel like precommitment behavior, a working group can stay with here-and-now processing, a characteristic of the commitment stage. Her concern is a fairly universal one; she wants to stay connected to the group, to continue the relationship. What do you think about group members staying in touch after group is over?

DR. FALL: A fear about the disconnection and loss of this experience.

AMANDA: Yeah.

KURT: I can relate to some of that. Recently, obviously some of my relationships haven't ended very well, but that's not normally how I am. Normally, I don't have much of a problem saying good-bye. I am kind of apprehensive about what's going to happen at this point, in this group. So, that's kind of what I'm feeling right now.

CHALI: My experience, I am thinking of one in particular right now, I am in the middle of saying good-bye to one of my roommates. She is leaving to go get married. It's a good thing, so I am excited for her, but at the same time, I am very sad for all the things I am losing from her relationship. The things she gave me like, she's the one when I say, "Let's go do this," she is down for anything all the time. I go to her for specific information and I'm going to lose that in her and that makes me really sad. I mean, I'm happy and sad at the same time and I guess that's how I feel about this group. You guys are, I don't know what the word is, but you are a wealth of knowledge that I can learn more about myself and learn how to be with other people, so that makes me sad, but happy because we can move on.

CAROLINE: Yeah, I have such mixed feelings about good-byes. I think about the last really big good-bye that I had was whenever I moved here for grad school. I was in a relationship, and we made the decision to break up, and it was just awful, and I really get what you are saying, like we can't speak. So, there was such a lack of resolution that I feel, to this day, even though it's been years. So on one hand, I get so nervous about it, but also with that, knowing that there were a lot of possibilities for me in that good-bye. Moving here and coming to grad school was the best decision I could have ever made and meeting someone new, who is perfect for me and fulfilling my dream in a city that I love. So, yeah, it's very bittersweet. Maybe it sounds too cliché. In here, I am so going to miss this, but I know that I am a better person for having been here, so it's a lot of really confusing stuff when I think about good-byes.

Dr. Fall: Yeah, mixed feelings.

Caroline: Definitely mixed feelings.

Chali and Caroline link over the ambivalent feelings that good-byes can produce. Here, the group members share experiences that demonstrate that good-byes can be productive, despite the complicated feelings. This is another fairly universal theme that will emerge and provides the group with a holistic perspective of good-bye feelings and outcomes that is more balanced than the "always good" or "always bad" approach.

Mallory: Well I definitely have mixed feelings as well because I feel like Caroline, we kind of came in with the same issue of balance, and I feel like she's helped me work through my problems and I can talk to her about it, but now, saying good-bye, as Amanda said, I can't just call her up on the phone because this is our group relationship, so I definitely have mixed feelings as well. I know it's going to be hard, but I feel like there is a good possibility of moving on and having more opportunities in the future based on what I've learned in this group.

Caroline: Thank you for that.

Greg: I could hitchhike on mixed feelings. As I think about us coming to an end, I have really appreciated everyone here in the group. You may have remembered I shared with you that I have a lot of history with good-byes because I am retired military. I have moved around a lot and have had to do a lot of good-byes, so good-byes have been just something that has been a part of my life a lot. I have experienced that. In terms of the good-bye experience, I am OK with being able to step away from situations, but this feels a little different. I have always been able to keep in touch with people I have wanted to keep in touch with when I said good-bye before, but we are going to go out in all different separate ways. We know each other here, but we don't know each other, as you said, we don't know each other outside of this environment. It's been great and I've enjoyed it. So, kind of mixed feelings about that. This is a different good-bye than what I've been dealing with before, for what it's worth.

Caroline: We can't recreate this experience even if we were to see each other outside.

Greg: That's a good point Caroline. So, we have to kind of step away from here and be on our own don't we?

Caroline: Yeah.

Greg: I hear you. I hear you.

Dr. Fall: And like you said, on one hand, it feels really good because it is empowering, and on the other hand it's sad to leave a meaningful experience and leave relationships behind. I am glad we had to process that and know where we stand with good-byes and be able to honor those mixed feelings because next week will be our good-bye. As a group, we are going to have to figure out how we are going to do that. We don't have to do that today. What I want you to do is honor the feelings you are having and just like we have done with everything else, we are going to decide as a group, next week, how we are going to bring this to a close. There may be times over the week, because of the mixed feelings, that you feel like maybe it's just better to not come. I want to encourage everyone, out of respect for the group, despite the feelings you might have, in spite of the fact it may be easier to not address it, to go ahead and have that last meeting. Beyond saying good-bye, it's also a time to tie up the work that we've done, to acknowledge the progress that we've made, to see what else needs to be done. It's also, for the rest of the time today, it would be good to think about what's left unsaid. What have you been needing to say to another group member that, for whatever reason you just haven't taken that chance or the opportunity just hasn't presented itself? Today is a good time to address that. So I wonder if there are any, as you are thinking about that, what comes up for you?

OK, there was quite a bit covered here. Dr. Fall uses a reflection to sum up the sharing experience of good-byes. He then transitions into discussing how the group will need to come up with a way to say good-bye for next week. This reinforces the thinking about the good-bye but also emphasizes the group responsibility for the process. Dr. Fall also foreshadows a very important dynamic about termination: members not showing up due to the complicated feelings. The discussion about good-byes helps limit the absences, but it is often a good idea to bring it up and encourage the members to attend regardless of what they might be feeling. Dr. Fall then addresses what can be done with the rest of the time in the present group. The focus here is on "tying up" the work. As the group moves to the end, it is normal for group members to try to bring up new issues (some would say as an effort to avoid terminating). The leader facilitates a constant movement towards the ending of the group. Dr. Fall does this by giving them something to focus on: a "last chance," so to speak, for resolving unfinished business.

MALLORY: Well, I haven't told Caroline, in depth, how thankful I am for her being able to share her experiences. When I am at home, and I see dishes piled up or the laundry piled up, homework papers, everything going on, I feel there are other people out in the world, not only Caroline, but through all of our experiences, I felt that everyone has helped me grow as a person in knowing that I am not alone.

Mallory provides a good example of the power of universality. Sometimes, just feeling that someone else in the world shares your pain can ease the anxiety of the presenting issue. Group counseling is a great place to experience this curative factor.

AMANDA: I wanted to share with Kurt, actually. Just in the last few sessions, really, I felt like you were pulling away. We've talked about, you know, like Greg's antennae, I just sensed that you were really pulling back and pulling away.
KURT: I guess, first of all, I am kind of surprised that you would say that. I wasn't aware of that. I am not exactly sure why. If it made you feel uncomfortable, I want to say I'm sorry. Maybe there are some unresolved things I'm trying to deal with here as we come to a close.
AMANDA: I kind of feel like you are doing it now.
KURT: OK. Well, like I said, maybe I am kind of feeling different as we are coming to a close right now. Maybe I am withdrawing from you a little bit. Maybe it's stemming from my trust issues. Recently, I haven't had a real good chance to say good-bye. I'm kind of mixed up about that, kind of dealing with that right now.

Amanda does a great job of trying to use the here and now to provide some feedback and address some unfinished business. She perceives Kurt is pulling back from the group and brings her feelings into the group. When Kurt responds somewhat defensively, she notes that he is pulling away in the here-and-now interaction with her. Kurt does respond and relates the struggle to his trust issues.

DR. FALL: What would you like Kurt to do, Amanda?

AMANDA: I guess . . .

DR. FALL: Tell him.

AMANDA: We talked before about how I really valued how here and present you were and how willing you were to engage, whether that meant you paying attention to all of us or giving of yourself. I haven't felt that, and I would love, you know, we still have today, and we have our last session, to have just as much of you here.

KURT: OK, OK. That is something I will definitely pay attention to in our last couple of sessions together. Thank you for bringing that up. I'll pay attention to that.

Hopefully you can see how Kurt is working on and making progress on his relationships through the interaction with Amanda. What is he learning about trust? What is he learning about himself in relationships?

DR. FALL: It's such a brilliant example of great feedback, of exactly what we were talking about. How the history of our good-byes and the connections, they impact us. I think what I heard you say is that you are sensing him moving away. It would make sense that as we are ending and you feel us moving away from you, that you are moving to protect yourself. But what I hear from Amanda is, she misses you and values that connection and wants you here so she can have, so you can have, so we can all have a real quality good-bye. It would be a different example from painful ones we have experienced in the past.

KURT: I think that makes sense. At least to me.

Reflection Questions

- How did this session meet with your expectations of a session before termination? What would you have done differently?

  _____

  _____

  _____

- How would you balance the leader's return to a more involved role with letting the group continue to facilitate the flow of the discussion? How did Dr. Fall balance these roles?

  _____

  _____

  _____

- The most shared perspective on good-byes was that of "mixed feelings." What else would you have done to explore this theme and prepare your group for termination?

  _____

  _____

  _____

- Hearing about members' experiences of good-byes can be another opportunity to use the "what does this look like in group?" filter. Discuss each member's perspective on good-byes and comment what that pattern would look like in group.

  _____

  _____

  _____

Segment 6

Termination

Introduction

Just as every group has a beginning, every group must end. However, the inevitable end does mean the group will have a healthy termination. I was called by an agency to consult on a series of psycho-educational groups they had been running every six weeks for about a year. They were pleased with the turn out for the groups, but members always complained at the end evaluation, and the most common negative comments contained the words, "no closure." For me, that meant termination might be an issue, so I asked how they ended the groups. The response from one of the leaders was, "We have our last group by having them fill out an evaluation, and once they are finished with the form, they leave." I am hopeful that you can see why these groups were having "closure" issues.

Termination is as important as any stage in the development of the group. As was mentioned in the last segment, almost everyone has experienced a painful, unresolved, confusing end to a relationship (or two), and group should be an opportunity to experience a healthy end. This segment demonstrates the process of terminating a group. You will notice the leader helping the group stay focused on the termination task, process growth, try to relate group learning to external learning, and the ritual of saying good-bye. The leader also continues the role of facilitator at the termination stage to monitor resistance and help guide the group through this final stage of development.

Preview Reflection Questions

- Review the ways group members often resist termination. Discuss how you, as a leader, would work with each method of resistance.

  _____

  _____

  _____

- The group was given the task to come up with a method of saying good-bye. In your opinion, what are some good rituals for saying good-bye? What would you do if the group came up with a way that you didn't think was appropriate for the group?

  _____

  _____

  _____

- How would you handle a situation where a member did not attend the last session?

  _____

  _____

  _____

Verbatim

DR. FALL: Welcome back to group. As we have been discussing, this is our last group together. Our last time. Thank you all for coming. We talked last time about good-byes and what that meant. Just to set the agenda for this week, as I mentioned, it will be a time to acknowledge the work that we've done, tie up any loose ends, and then find a way, as a group, that we can say good-bye, that will bring closure to this experience. One way to acknowledge the work that we've done is to think and talk a little bit about, I don't know, something that you feel like you gave to the group during your time here and maybe something that you got from the group. Just your thoughts on that.

Dr. Fall is setting the parameters of the termination session, which will increase the probability of the group staying on task to terminate. Having the group discuss what each person gave and gained from the group is a nice way to focus the group and bring a sense of growth and completion to the experience. What are some other ideas of activities that might fulfill the same goal?

MALLORY: Well, I feel what I gave to the group were my experiences of being a woman and interacting with the traditional roles of the male and female and how we could relate that to each other's experiences. What I really took from the group was everyone's experiences of how to balance your time and how you handle conflicting roles and how to not get so stressed out when you feel you have so much stuff to do, by prioritizing and time management, making a calendar and setting all of your time up.

DR. FALL: So you found some practical ways to utilize the information in relationships.

This is a good example of the curative factor of vicarious learning and how it operates in group. If you notice, we did not spend time in group brainstorming about how Mallory could solve her balance issue. Instead, by focusing on the theme of balance, Mallory learned about how to balance by listening to other group members struggle with balance as well. As she processed and listened to the struggle, she also heard other ways of achieving balance in her life.

GREG: Well, you know, in terms of what I gave to the group, Caroline, I remember you saying, that you said earlier, that you were real uncomfortable with conflict. I remember that. Do you remember that? I remember though that we were able to interact, you and I, and talk through some uncomfortable stuff as we stepped through there. Kind of what I gave to the group and what I got from the group, they both tie in because I hope that was something that was value added for you as we stepped through there. I'll tell you what I got from the group is being able to do that. What I got from the group is being able to talk to you guys. As I came in here in the beginning I told you about racial differences and how intensely sometimes I can feel different. It doesn't mean I walk out of here and all of a sudden feel like I am the same, but it definitely helps me to walk out of here and feel better about being able to interact and just have a chance to talk about it with you guys. In this laboratory, for lack of a better description, it really helped. So, I got that from all of you and I really appreciate it.

DR. FALL: You know, I've been thinking a lot about our discussion about feeling disconnected and I think over our time together I think what I figured out was whenever I heard you, in the first group, say that you felt different, I automatically thought that that meant that you wanted to be less different and I think that was a mistake that I made. One of the things that I think you have done and taught me here, and you just said it, is that you are not any less different than when you started. None of us are. We are each the same person as when we began and we are all different. You are no different from when you began but you are more connected than when you began. I think that is what I missed. You were asking to be less different. You are asking to be more connected, accepted and heard.

GREG: Yeah, that talks to me. I like that.

DR. FALL: So, I wasn't going to participate, but that's what I got from the group.

GREG: I appreciate that.

Dr. Fall uses immediacy to not only participate in the closing activity, but also to model the courage to be imperfect by admitting a "mistake." It is important for counselors to not only be comfortable with imperfection but to also model it to their clients and group members. It can decrease the intensity of viewing the counselor as an almighty expert and can diminish the norm of perfection, which can limit group sharing.

CHALI: Going on that, I think I gave that connection and that ability to connect with you and connect with everyone here. I really opened myself up for that and I think I gave that and hopefully you guys felt that just like he did. Something I got was just the bravery of everyone sharing. Being OK with sharing, "Hey, this is what I experienced," like with you Greg and you Mallory. And how you, Amanda, last week you were saying, "Hey Kurt, I've been experiencing you this way." Sometimes I have been scared to do that in the past. I have this second-guessing, and I have become more OK with saying, "OK, there is second-guessing in my head and if I really need to I can check with someone else." I can really check with them and see that's really true or if it's just me in my head or whatever. I'm thankful that you guys shared your bravery with me and I've learned from that.

CAROLINE: I'll go. This is going to sound kind of weird so I hope it comes across the way it sounds in my head. I think what I gave to this group was my presence. It was really a battle to not let this become another item on the to-do list, and there were many weeks when I just felt so overwhelmed and I wanted to give in to that stuck feeling, but I still came and was here, and that to me was a really big deal. Kind of along those same lines, the thing that I got from this is I got to see that I can power through that feeling of being paralyzed in the midst of everything that is going on to very positive results instead of just hanging out on the couch and feeling "Woe is me, and I can't do anything, and this is too overwhelming." I could do something and not even something on my to-do list, but something that takes care of me, and that made a lot of difference.

AMANDA: I think we are all having the same experience, where we are like, "Well, I gave . . ." and it's sort of hard to say, and I'm not sure why, but I noticed it with all of us. What I gave mostly is just coming and caring about every week and carrying that out throughout the week because it would have been really easy to switch into that mode, just when I got here, because I don't see any of you otherwise, but processing the topics that we covered throughout the week, not just in myself, but also caring about the growth everyone else is having. That's also what I got from the group was hearing everyone's issues throughout the week and how we are growing and what we are experiencing and taking that home. That really helped get me out of myself. My big issues were figuring out who I am and how to represent that, and I was really helped by the fact I had other things to care about than worrying about myself.

Amanda's perspective is interesting in that it provides an example of the curative factor of altruism; gaining a sense of growth through helping and caring for others. One of the benefits of altruism is that it helps individuals avoid the dynamic of morbid self-absorption. When Amanda talks about, "I was really helped by the fact I had other things to care about than worrying about myself," she is illustrating the power of altruism. This curative factor is unique to group.

KURT: As far as thinking about what I gave to the group, I'd like to think that I gave effort. I came to the group every week hoping that I could share some things about myself and also learn about others. From week to week, I tried my best to be attentive and to listen to others as well as to share some difficulties of some things I am going through. I'm not sure exactly how that came out to everybody, if you all felt that way at times, but I wanted to say I did try, and I did give effort. That's what I think I gave to the group. As far as getting, what I got from the group, I think it's going to take some time to realize what I really took and what I learned from this group, but I do want to say that I've learned a lot over the time that we've been meeting with one another. I felt good that people listened to me. I think just the camaraderie that I built with some of you, I think it really helped with my trust issues. I do trust y'all, and that means a lot to me, and I'm going to try to bring the trust that I've formed with y'all into my life and we'll see that how that progresses as time goes on.

Dr. Fall: You know, I remember the first group meeting when you talked about your particular issue, and I got so excited, from a group-leader perspective, because that issue of working on trust is such a great, natural, goal to have. The reason why I got so excited is because it is not something that you can just talk about. I knew that through the life of the group, that if we did what we needed to do and you were active, then you would make progress. That something would happen because this was about relationships. I hope what you all take from this, and building off your issue, is interpersonal issues like trust or feeling different and wanting to be connected or being understood, balancing, it's not a passive process. It's an active process. So if you think about all the growth you made, it's not from sitting back and observing. It was about taking a risk and getting out there and making something happen. So that process of connection actually did a lot of good for each one of your goals.

Dr. Fall attempts to address issues of universality and active participation in the growth process as additive dynamics in group. These statements could also be made at the beginning of the group process to help motivate and orient members to the process of group. In this case, the statements are used as a summarizing statement and are meant to orient and motivate the members to recognizing and continuing their growth as they move back into the external world.

Dr. Fall: One of the things we did discuss is that we have to come up with a way to say good-bye as a group to bring the issues of this group to a close. As I said, we are going to decide this as a group and see what feels right for us. Any ideas?

This is the transition into closing the group. In this group, the leader mentioned that the group would decide on how to end the group. You want to make sure you leave enough time in the group to discuss, decide, and enact the closing activity.

Caroline: I think I might have one. Something that really stuck with me from the first session that I thought at the time would be really silly but it ended up being pretty powerful was we had a moment at the end of the first session to just look at each person and look them in the eyes and think of something that we learned about them. I still go back to that and still try to do that and think each time, "What am I learning about this person?" I think I would really love to end where we began in a sense.

Dr. Fall: To come full circle?

Caroline: Yeah.

Kurt: That's a great idea Caroline.

Dr. Fall: Any objections to that?

Greg: I think it sounds pretty good.

MALLORY: I think it sounds like a good idea . . . like a new beginning.

CHALI: [*Laughing and singing*] I keep thinking, "The circle of life . . ." [*Group laughs.*]

DR. FALL: It's neat because it's an experience we all had. We'll take the last few minutes that we have in group, and, much like we did the first time, I want you to make sure you make eye contact with each person, and that will be your way of saying good-bye. I don't know if I want to put any stipulations on what it is you think of when you make eye contact with that person. It might be what you gave that person, what you got from them, or whatever you need to do to close out that relationship. You will close it when you break eye contact and move on to the next person. When all that is done, we will be done and we will leave. So, go ahead and start.

Caroline comes up with an idea, and Dr. Fall facilitates consensus within the group. He also allows the group members some freedom in how they say their good-byes, in this case, what they are thinking while making eye contact, but also explains the process enough to decrease the possibility of some members feeling lost within the activity. As with any activity, he explains how to begin, how to proceed, and how to end.

Reflection Questions

• What is your overall reaction to the termination session? What would you have done differently?

_____

_____

_____

• What do you think will be the most difficult part of terminating a group? What can you do, as a leader, to manage this difficulty?

_____

_____

_____

• Dr. Fall, in a way, participated in the termination activity by sharing his thoughts with Greg. What do you think about leaders participating in group activities? When is it appropriate? When might it be inappropriate?

_____

_____

_____

- In responding to Kurt, Dr. Fall comments that he was excited when Kurt brought up his issue because, "I knew that through the life of the group, that if we did what we needed to do and you were active, then you would make progress. That something would happen because this was about relationships." What do you think he meant by this?

_____

_____

_____